Shaping
Materials

Chris Oxlade

 Crabtree Publishing Company
www.crabtreebooks.com

Crabtree Publishing Company

www.crabtreebooks.com

Editors: Hayley Leach, Adrianna Morganelli, Michael Hodge
Senior Design Manager: Rosamund Saunders
Designer: Ben Ruocco
Photographer: Philip Wilkins

Photo credits: 1Apix/Alamy p. 6, Chris Alack/Getty Images
p. 17, Tim Caddick/Alamy p. 23, Darrin Jenkins/Alamy p. 16,
Fortune fish/Alamy p. 12, Jeff Morgan/Alamy p. 11, Janine
Wiedel Photolibrary /Alamy p. 21, Xela/Alamy p. 15, Ute
Kaiser/zefa/Corbis p. 7, Michael Keller/Corbis p. 9, Tom
Stewart/Corbis cover and p. 20, Paul Jones/Getty Images
p. 13, Jeremy Liebman/Getty Images p. 10, Joel
Sartore/National Geographic/Getty Images p. 19, Chris Oxlade
p. 14, Richard Jung/Photolibrary.com p. 8, Peter
Weimann/Photolibrary.com p. 24, Steve Allen/Science Photo
Library p. 18, R. Maisonneuve, Publiphoto Diffusion/Science
Photo Library p. 25, Rosenfield Images Ltd/Science Photo
Library p. 22, Philip Wilkins pp. 26-27.

Activity & illustrations: Shakespeare Squared pp. 28-29.

Cover: A potter is using clay to make a pot.

Title page: A worker uses a chisel to shape a stone archway.

The publishers would like to thank the models Philippa and
Sophie Campbell for appearing in the photographs.

Because of the nature of the Internet, it is possible that
some website addresses (URLs) included in this book may
have changed, or sites may have changed or closed down
since publication. While the author and publisher regret any
inconvenience this may cause the readers, no responsibility
for any such changes can be accepted by either the author
or the publisher.

Library and Archives Canada Cataloguing in Publication

Oxlade, Chris
    Shaping materials / Chris Oxlade.

(Working with materials)
Includes index.
ISBN 978-0-7787-3641-7 (bound).--ISBN 978-0-7787-3651-6 (pbk.)

    1. Materials--Juvenile literature. 2. Materials--Experiments--
Juvenile
literature. I. Title. II. Series: Oxlade, Chris. Working with materials.

TA403.2.O95 2007   j620.1'1   C2007-904319-4

Library of Congress Cataloging-in-Publication Data

Oxlade, Chris.
    Shaping materials / Chris Oxlade.
      p. cm. -- (Working with materials)
    Includes index.
    ISBN-13: 978-0-7787-3641-7 (rlb)
    ISBN-10: 0-7787-3641-5 (rlb)
    ISBN-13: 978-0-7787-3651-6 (pb)
    ISBN-10: 0-7787-3651-2 (pb)
    1. Materials--Juvenile literature. 2. Materials--Experiments--Juvenile
literature. I. Title. II. Series.

    TA403.2.O953 2007
    620.1'1--dc22

                           2007027422

Crabtree Publishing Company

www.crabtreebooks.com   1-800-387-7650

Published in Canada
Crabtree Publishing
616 Welland Ave.
St. Catharines, Ontario
L2M 5V6

Published in the United States
Crabtree Publishing
PMB16A
350 Fifth Ave., Suite 3308
New York, NY 10118

CONTENTS

Words in **bold** can be found in the glossary on page 30

Shaping materials

Everything around you is made up of materials. Everyday materials include paper, plastic, metal, and glass. We use these materials to make objects such as tables, chairs, shoes, cars, and aircraft.

↓ *All of these objects are plastic. They were made by putting liquid plastic into **molds**.*

6

← A dressmaker is cutting a piece of fabric into the shape she wants using a pair of scissors.

Some materials come in blocks or sheets. Others come as liquids or powders. Cutting, folding, and molding are some ways of shaping materials into objects. The method that we use depends on the **properties** of the material.

Scissors and saws

Cutting with scissors is a simple way to make shapes from materials such as paper and fabric. A pair of scissors has two sharp blades that slice through the material.

↓ This cook is cutting pastry shapes. The pastry cutter has a sharp metal blade.

← *This **carpenter** is cutting a piece of wood with a saw to make the shape that he wants.*

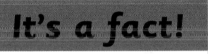

It's a fact!

When saw blades are made, they are heated and then dipped in water. This makes them extra hard.

We cut through thick pieces of material, such as wood, with a saw. A saw blade has hundreds of sharp grooves called "teeth". As the saw moves backward and forward, the teeth rip away tiny bits of material.

Carving materials

An artist can make a wooden sculpture by carving a block of wood. The artist cuts bits off of the block using a knife or a sharp tool called a chisel. It takes a lot of skill to cut away the right bits.

↓ *An artist is shaping wood with a chisel.*

↑ *A stone mason chips away stone*
  with a hammer and chisel.

Artists called stone masons work
with stone. They start with a block
of stone and gradually chip away
pieces to make the shape that they
want. We also shape stone blocks to
make the walls of buildings.

It's a fact!

The ancient Egyptians
built giant stone
pyramids using
thousands of stone
blocks. Workers cut
the blocks using simple
hand tools.

Folding and bending

We can make objects by folding and bending flat sheets of material. For example, we make envelopes and paper bags by folding paper. Cardboard boxes are made by folding stiff cardboard.

← *You can make shapes, such as this flower, by folding a piece of paper.*

↑ *This tent has metal poles. The poles are bent over to make the dome shape of the tent.*

Bending lets us make rounded shapes from flat sheets of materials. For example, shoes are made by bending leather around a wooden block called a "last".

It's a fact!

A curved wooden chair seat is made by bending flat sheets of wood. The wood is heated with steam to make it easier to bend.

Machine shapers

Many objects are shaped by machines. The machines have blades that cut away material from a block. This leaves the shape that is wanted.

← This machine cuts wood into shapes. The blade in the middle spins to cut away the wood.

↑ *A carpenter is making*
an ornament on a lathe.

Carpenters and metalworkers often
use a machine called a "lathe".
It makes round objects, such as rods
and poles. The material spins around
at a high speed. A blade cuts away
the material.

It's a fact!

Computers control
machines to make
objects such as nuts
and bolts. The computer
automatically moves the
material and the blades
to cut the shape.

Molding materials

Chocolates, ice cubes, and bowls all have something in common. They are all made in a mold. A mold has a **hollow** space inside. The hollow space is the shape of the object being made.

↓ Chocolate is warmed to make it soft. Then it is poured into molds. It gets hard again when it cools.

← Jellies are made by putting a warm jelly mixture into a mold. The jelly turns solid when it cools.

Runny material is poured into the mold.
It fills the mold to make a new object.
The runny material gradually gets hard.
Then the object is taken out of the mold.
Now the mold is ready to be used again.

Molding in industry

Nearly all plastic items are made by molding. The plastic is warmed to make it soft. Then it is put into a mold. When the plastic cools, the object is taken out of the mold. Glass objects are also made in molds.

↓ *This plastic can has just been taken out of its mold.*

18

↑ *This is molten copper. It is being poured into a mold.*

Some metal objects are made in molds. The metal is heated up until it melts. The **molten** metal is poured into a mold. When the metal cools, it turns solid again.

It's a fact!

Builders use molds to make concrete shapes. They build wooden molds and then pour concrete in. When the concrete is hard, they take away the wood.

19

Shaping soft materials

Some materials are easy to shape when they are very soft. Potter's clay is very soft. You can easily shape it with your hands. A potter uses simple tools to shape clay.

← This potter is using her hands to shape a clay pot.

↑ *This glass blower is making a glass vase by
blowing air into a blob of hot, soft glass.*

Glass is normally very hard, and it
can break easily. Glass gets soft when
it is heated. Glass blowers shape glass
with special tools when it is hot. Then
they let the glass cool and get hard.

It's a fact!

Soft materials, such as
cake icing, can be
pushed through a
small hole. This
makes a long, thin
piece of material.

Shaping metals

Iron, steel, **aluminum**, and copper are all types of metal. They are strong and hard. We shape metals by cutting and molding them.

↓ *This machine is cutting a sheet of metal using a **laser**.*

← *This machine is pressing a metal object into shape.*

It's a fact!

The round shape of a coin is cut from a sheet of metal. Then another machine presses the picture onto each side of the coin.

We can squash, stretch, bend, and twist a piece of metal. We make objects such as metal bowls and can lids by pressing sheets of metal into shape.

Hammering and rolling metals

A blacksmith makes items, such as **horseshoes** and garden gates, from iron. The blacksmith heats up the iron. This makes the iron softer and easier for the blacksmith to hammer into shape.

↓ *A blacksmith is making a horseshoe. He is working on a heavy block of iron called an "anvil".*

↑ *Copper is rolled into sheets.*

Thin sheets of metal, such as steel, are made by rollers. The metal starts as a block. The metal is heated to make it easier to roll. It goes through many rollers. It gradually gets thinner and thinner.

It's a fact!

Metal wire is used to make things like paper clips. Wire is made by stretching a piece of metal a bit at a time. The metal gets thinner and longer.

See for yourself!

Molding ice shapes

Create your own molds to make different ice shapes.

What you need	
modeling clay	water
plastic food wrap	small object (such as a
old saucer	toy building block)

① Flatten a large lump of modeling clay until it is about 1 inch (2.5 cm) thick and about 3 inches (8 cm) across.

② Lay a piece of plastic food wrap loosely over the top of the modeling clay.

③ Press an object firmly into the top of the modeling clay. Now take it off again. You have made a mold of the object.

④ Put the mold on a saucer. Carefully fill the mold with water.

⑤ Put the saucer in the freezer.

⑥ When frozen, carefully take the ice out of the mold. You have made a copy of the object out of ice.

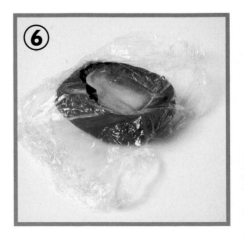

Making a box

Find out how to make a box by cutting and folding.

What you need

pencil   scissors
ruler   adhesive tape
paper

① Copy the pattern here onto a piece
of paper. Cut along the solid lines.
Do not cut along the dotted lines.

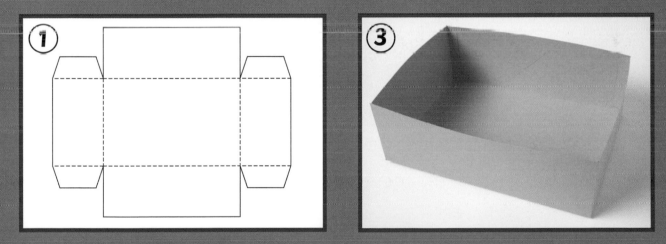

② Bend the paper along all of the dotted
lines. Fold all of the side panels up, and
then fold the end tabs around.

③ Using adhesive tape, attach the end tabs
to the side panels. You have made a box.

Beautiful butterflies

Making pipe cleaner butterflies

Fold and bend simple materials into beautiful butterflies!

What you need
colorful construction paper or tissue paper
pencil
colorful pipe cleaners
scissors
ruler

1. Choose two pieces of construction paper or tissue paper. Using a ruler, trace a 5-inch (13-cm) square on one sheet and a 4-inch (10-cm) square on the other. Cut out both squares.

2. Accordion-fold each square on its diagonal.

3. Bend a pipe cleaner in half, creating a small loop on the bottom.

4. Pinch the center of each square to form a bow-tie shape. Arrange the squares inside the folded pipe cleaner, with the bow-tie center in the middle. Place the larger square above the smaller one. These are the butterfly's wings.

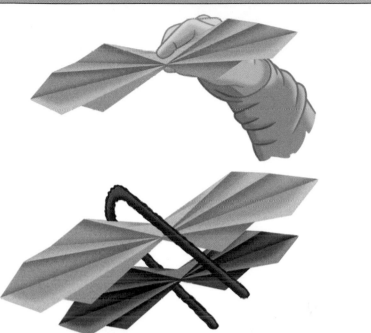

5. Twist the pipe cleaner above and below each pinched square to keep the wings in place.

6. Make antennae by curling the top ends of the pipe cleaner.

What you will see:
You have now created your own butterfly! You shaped the wings by folding paper, and you shaped the body and antennae by bending and twisting a pipe cleaner. The wire inside the pipe cleaner helped it keep its shape. What other animals can you create from pipe cleaners and paper?

Glossary

aluminum A type of metal that is strong but lightweight

carpenter A person who makes things from wood

horseshoe A curved piece of iron that gets nailed to a horse's foot

hollow An empty space inside a mold

laser A device that makes a beam of light

molten When something is heated until it melts

mold To make an object into a mold

runny When something flows like a liquid, such as water

property Tells us what a material is like. The hardness of a material and how easily it melts are examples of properties

Further information

BOOKS

How We Use: Metals/Paper/Rubber/Wood
by Chris Oxlade, Raintree (2005)

A Material World: It's Glass/It's Metal/It's Plastic/It's Wood
by Kay Davies and Wendy Oldfield, Wayland (2006)

Investigating Science: How do we use materials?
by Jacqui Bailey, Franklin Watts (2005)

WEBSITES

www.bbc.co.uk/schools/revisewise/science/materials/09_act.shtml
Animated examples and quiz about changing materials

www.strangematterexhibit.com
Fun site about the properties of materials

PLACES TO VISIT

American Museum of Science and Energy, Tennessee
www.amse.org

The Children's Museum of Science and Technology, New York
www.cmost.com

The Discovery Center for Science and Technology, California
www.discoverycntr.org

Index

All of the numbers in **bold** refer to photographs

Printed in the USA